CRAZY STUFF
MINNESOTA

LITTLE-KNOWN FACTS ABOUT THE
LAND OF 10,000 LAKES

CLIFF ROAD
BOOKS

**CLIFF ROAD
BOOKS**

Crazy Stuff Minnesota

Copyright © 2009 Cliff Road Books, Inc.

ISBN-13: 9781602613645

Book design by Miles G. Parsons
Illustrations by Tim Rocks
Text by Larisa Lovelady

Printed in China

TABLE OF CONTENTS

CRAZY GUYS & GALS

The Roseville Area Schools' list of 2008 high school seniors included a 93-year-old man, Harold Pugh, who was awarded an honorary diploma to recognize him for his lifetime achievements. Pugh dropped out of high school to join the merchant marines and served in the Army during World War II. He earned the Purple Heart on D-Day, June 6, 1944, when he was shot twice. When he returned home, he took a job with the U.S. Postal Service and was never able to finish high school. He worked for the postal service for almost 40 years and is a now dance instructor.

◆

In October 2007, with the help of her cane, 93-year-old Lucille Keppen walked away from her 4-year tenure as Minnesota's oldest prisoner. Her release date coincided with what would have been her late husband's 104th birthday, and she celebrated with friends by having a large breakfast at a local restaurant. Keppen was incarcerated at the women's correctional facility in Shakopee, Minnesota, following a guilty plea to first-degree assault when she shot her caretaker, a 64-year-old man, in the back because he noticed other women.

◆

Hutchinson resident Milburn Henke made history on January 26, 1942, when he became the first United States combat soldier to land in Europe during World War II. Newspapers nationwide carried the image of Henke arriving in Belfast, Ireland.

◆

Two Minnesotans' summer 2006 expedition to the North Pole by canoe and skis was the first of its kind. Grand

Marais residents Lonnie Dupre and Eric Larson were the first to make the unusual summer trip and did so to bring attention to global warming.

◆

The 2006 U.S. Scrabble Open was won by 48-year-old Jim Kramer of Roseville, Minnesota. Kramer won $25,000 along with the championship Scrabble title.

◆

Minnesota native Walter Breuning celebrated his 112th birthday in September 2008. As of his birthday, Breuning was the 27th oldest person in the world.

St. Paul's Regions Hospital set a hospital record on July 10, 2008, when 16 babies were born in a 17-hour period. Eight boys and eight girls pushed their way into the record book on what is reportedly one of the busiest days for births each year.

◆

Lynn and Ralph Pierre were married in 1977 and have raised three children in their home in a cemetery. Lynn has been quoted as saying that the big backyard and peacefulness of the cemetery make it a fine place to raise a family. The Pierre family lives and works at Union Cemetery in Maplewood.

MyWonderfulLife.com is a Web site that provides free resources for personalized funeral planning. The site was launched by two Minnesota women and includes a printable one-page summary intended as a reference for relatives of the deceased to carry out last wishes.

◆

Raleane Kupferschmidt, a 65-year-old St. Elmo woman, was brought home from the hospital to die after doctors said she had no brain activity and would never recover from a coma. As her family and friends began saying their last good-byes, she woke up and steadily recovered.

Jason Patton, a Minnesota pilot, was unharmed after he jumped from the cockpit of his experimental plane moments before the plane spun out, hit the ground, and caught fire in November of 2008.

◆

A Winona woman called firefighters to rescue her when she got her hand stuck in her toilet. She was trying to remove a deodorant container that had fallen in.

◆

A state police helicopter, 50 rescuers, strapped-together canoes, hovercraft, and amphibious vehicles were used to safely pull 500-pound Pine City resident Martin Rike from Wisconsin's St. Croix River in 2007. Rike was stuck in shoals for more than 12 hours after the innertube he was riding deflated, and he began having chest pains.

◆

The voice of a Minnesota teenager has been heard millions of times worldwide via a YouTube video called "Dancing." Palbasha Siddique from Bangladesh moved with her family to Minneapolis in 2001 when MacPhail Center for the Arts awarded her a scholarship. Siddique's voice was discovered by the creators of the video through a radio interview on Minneapolis's KFAI-FM. During the interview, she sang a few lines from a song called "Praan," which means "life" in Bengali. The "Dancing" video's creators, upon hearing Siddique sing, recruited her immediately to accompany jig-dancing Minnesotan Matt Harding as he performs his quirky routine with people worldwide, with monkeys, and underwater.

◆

Marguerite Meyers, 83, and Leonard Firlick, 90, of Eagan, Minnesota, married about a year after they met at church—and after they signed a prenuptial agreement.

Minnesota was home to Kathleen E. Woodiwiss, the creator of the modern historical romance novel, who passed away in Minneapolis in 2007 after introducing the romance writing genre to the world and publishing 13 novels in 35 years.

◆

In 2007, a 45-year-old woman in St. Paul posted most of her worldly possessions for sale in one auction on eBay for a reserve bid of $2,000. Furniture, clothes, books, electronics, and kitchen utensils were among the items included in Lisa Perry's auction that she conducted prior to relocating to California.

Queen Elizabeth II awarded an Honorary Commander of the Most Excellent Order of the British Empire to Minneapolis resident Sheila Leatherman. Leatherman received the award, which is given to non-British citizens, in 2007 for her work to reform Britain's health care system, including research on health care quality.

◆

A 70-year-old Minnesota woman has been working on a school assignment for 57 years. In January 1951, Marlene Yeomans, who lives in England, began a pen pal correspondence with Karen Sorensen, who lives in Minnesota, as part of an assignment at school. The women both say that they feel like sisters because of their pen pal relationship. They have traveled to meet each other three times since their correspondence began.

◆

A Minnesota prison inmate filed a $77,000 lawsuit against American Express because the company refused to return the only copy of a book manuscript he sent to them for comment, although American Express said they returned it promptly. The book explained how the prisoner defrauded American Express out of thousands of dollars in credit card charges, which resulted in his conviction and subsequent prison term.

The Arneson family of Red Wing boasts two winners of *Hockey Moms* magazine's Minnesota Mullet Contest. Their younger son Brady won in 2008 at age 3, and their older son Blake won in 2005.

CRAZY HISTORY

The world's largest twine ball rolled by one man was 29 years in the making and now resides in an acrylic gazebo in Darwin, Minnesota. It was started in March of 1950 by Francis A. Johnson, who wrapped it daily for 4 hours.

An 1857 bill to make St. Peter Minnesota's state capital was never passed because the bill was stolen.

◆

Since its inception in 1849, the Minncsota State Law Library has been located in a former Ford Motor Company factory and showroom, a hotel, a market, a log tavern, in three state capitol buildings, as well as its current location, the Minnesota Judicial Center.

◆

Known as the Taconite Capital of the World, Mountain Iron is home to U.S. Steel's Minntac plant, which is the world's largest taconite processing plant.

Madison is known as the Lutefisk Capital of the United States and is home to a statue of a giant cod named Lou T. Fisk. The 25-foot fiberglass fish has not been content to remain on his pedestal in J.F. Jacobson Park. Instead, he can routinely be seen in local parades on a travel trailer and even toured the country to observe President James Madison's 236th birthday. Following a makeover at the company where he was manufactured, he returned to his post on Highway 75, where he welcomes visitors to Madison.

◆

Karlstad is known as the Moose Capital of the North.

Minnesota, which became the 32nd state
of the United States on May 11, 1858, is
the country's 12th state in terms of land
area.

◆

The state beer designation was contested
in 1987 when both Schell's Deer Brand
and Cold Spring were proposed. Neither
was selected, but milk was adopted as the
official state drink in 1984.

◆

In 1984, Minnesota distinguished itself as
the first state to have an official state
mushroom. The morel mushroom
(*Morchella esculenta*) is also known as
the honeycomb morel or the sponge

mushroom. This fungus is particularly prized by mushroom hunters.

◆

Savage, Minnesota, is named for entrepreneur Marion Willis Savage, who used newspapers, posters, and flyers to promote a racehorse he owned named Dan Patch. The horse's fame grew to such an extent worldwide that his hometown of Hamilton changed its name to Savage to honor the fortunate owner. Dan Patch Drive and Dan Patch Lane in Savage now give tribute to the record-setting horse.

◆

In 2007, Minnesota joined a few other states in adopting an official state muffin.

Minnesota's choice was blueberry. A recipe for this state symbol is featured on the Web site of the Minnesota Secretary of State. Some unofficial Minnesota state symbols that have been proposed for consideration include: the Tilt-A-Whirl (amusement ride), licorice (candy), leech (parasite), lester loam (soil).

◆

St. Paul has been called a lot of names. American Indians called the area White Rock. Later it was known as Fountain Cave. For a while, it was referred to as Lambert's Landing after Colonel George Lambert, who worked to modernize navigation on the Upper Mississippi. The most imaginative option: Pig's Eye, after a famous local tavern.

Eveleth, Minnesota, is home to the world's largest hockey stick, which is 110 feet long and weighs 10,000 pounds. It cost $60,000 and was built in 2002 to replace the old stick, which lasted 7 years.

◆

Minnesota lakes are a treasure trove of archaeology. Bison bones with an imbedded arrowhead were once found by a boy as he swam. A sport diver, diving near Grand Portage, reported stone igloos or rings that are believed to be an early American Indian lodge now submerged in Lake Superior's waters.

Among other artifacts, Minnesota lakes have produced dugout canoes, flat-bottom ricing boats, and the remains of birchbark canoes and paddles.

CRAZY INVENTIONS & BUSINESSES

The first experimental water skis were made out of barrel staves and a long window sash, and were used to ride the waters of Lake Pepin. Eighteen-year-old Ralph Samuelson and his brother, Ben, were the inventors of the sport in 1922

when Ralph said, "If you can ski on snow, then you can ski on water." Three years later, Ralph used a greased 4-by-16-foot ramp to make the first water ski jump. The American Water Ski Association officially declared Samuelson the Father of Water Skiing at its 1972 meeting. Despite Ralph's claim to fame, his water skiing equipment was never patented.

◆

The first United States company to offer a money-back guarantee was Plainview's J.R. Watkins Medical Co., which continues to produce its first product, Watkins Red Liniment.

More than half of the wool blankets and throws produced in the United States are made in Faribault at the Faribault Woolen Mill, which was founded in 1865.

◆

To get booth space he needed to market his invention at cat shows, St. Paul's Edward Lowe cleaned hundreds of cat boxes in exchange for being allowed to show his product. Lowe's 1947 invention was dubbed Kitty Litter.

◆

Scotch tape was named by an auto painter who said that the frugal, or Scotch, managers at 3M Co. needed to add more adhesive to their masking and cellophane adhesive tapes. The product originally only had adhesive on the edges. The company capitalized on the new name by introducing a new mascot in 1944, Scotty McTape, and the next year, the now-familiar tartan package appeared.

◆

Scotchgard was invented in 1953 when a lab assistant at 3M in St. Paul dropped a glass bottle of synthetic latex on a canvas tennis shoe. The latex wouldn't wash off and couldn't be removed with solvent. The latex was made by Minneapolis native and research chemist Patsy Sherman.

Henry Neils, the owner of Flour City Ornamental Iron Co. in Minneapolis, made the first aluminum boats in 1946. The boats were manufactured under the Alumacraft name and were revolutionary, because at the time, most recreational boats were made of wood. Neils used his staff of skilled metalworkers and the aluminum surplus he had when World War II ended to make the boats.

CRAZY FOOD

Crazy Legs Conti ate 24 hot dogs in 12 minutes at the Nathan's Mall of America 2007 Regional Hot Dog Eating Contest.

◆

Some of Minnesota's most famous eating contests feature corn, sauerkraut, strawberry pie, White Castle burgers, pasta, Buffalo Wild Wings, Scotch eggs, and Black Forest torte.

◆

An Ely, Minnesota, couple is selling Crapola! across the United States. Crapola! is cranberry-apple granola cereal that combines organic grains, nuts, dried cranberries, apples, maple syrup, honey, and large amounts of humor to "make even really weird people regular."

◆

The technologies that spurred the development of Cheerios and Kix breakfast cereals were developed by Minnesota physicist Lester Borchardt. Borchardt was a General Mills employee for 36 years and invented a new way of closing cereal bags, as well as a device for measuring the moisture content of wheat kernels. Borchardt passed away in Minneapolis in 2007 at the age of 99.

◆

The world's largest cupcake was created at the Mall of America in Minneapolis in March 2008 by Duff Goldman, star of *Ace of Cakes* on Food Network. Goldman used 3 ounces of food coloring, 10 pounds of sugar, and 16 pounds of butter to create the 61.4-pound confection. The entirely edible cupcake measured more than a foot tall and was estimated to be about 150 times larger than a regular cupcake. The record was quickly rescinded when *Guinness World Records* learned that the gigantic cupcake had been constructed in two parts.

◆

The likenesses of the 12 finalists of the annual Princess Kay of the Milky Way contest are carved from 90 pound blocks of butter each year during the Minnesota State Fair. Fairgoers can watch the carving process, which takes about 8 hours to complete.

◆

Culinary meets convenience at the Minnesota State Fair, where an enormous variety of foods are carried and eaten on a stick. On-a-stick fair options include:

teriyaki-ostrich-on-a-stick, cheesecake-on-a-stick, fried-fruit-on-a-stick, pork-chop-on-a-stick, fried-candy-bar-on-a-stick, lamb-on-a-stick, walleye-on-a-stick, nut-rolls-on-a-stick, rocky-road scones-on-a-stick, macaroni-and-cheese-on-a-stick, spaghetti-on-a-stick, s'mores-on-a-stick, alligator-on-a-stick, pie-on-a-stick, sloppy-joe-on-a-stick, and fried-bacon-on-a-stick caramelized with maple syrup.

◆

Kool-Aid pickles (pickles soaked in Kool-Aid), foot-long walleye sandwiches, peanut butter hot dogs, and elk burgers have been included in the Minnesota Sate Fair's list of foods without a stick.

Superhero costumed servers deliver pizza in electric-powered cars at Galactic Pizza, a Minneapolis restaurant that uses wind-powered electricity for its pizza ovens.

◆

Chanhassen Dinner Theater, the nation's largest professional dinner theater with a seating capacity of 600, celebrated 40 years of combining theater productions and meals in 2008.

CRAZY NATURE

Whiplash the monkey was knighted by the king and queen of the Winter Carnival at the World's Toughest Rodeo in St. Paul, Minnesota, in 2009. Whiplash was born in 1987 and is most often seen dressed in a red vest and riding on a Border collie.

Lakota the wolf stole backpacks, pizzas, sweatshirts, water bottles, and a stuffed toy moose during the 15 years she lived at the International Wolf Center in Ely.

◆

"A wave of hundreds of minnows" hit Joe Saboe's roof in Dawson, Minnesota, in July, 1995. Saboe speculated that they were brought in by a waterspout from the nearby Minnesota River.

◆

The 2008 Frazee Turkey Days celebration attracted Twin City residents and one wild black bear with a clear plastic jug stuck on its head. Wildlife officials had been trying to trap

and tranquilize the bear since it was
spotted 6 days prior to his Turkey Days
debut. The jug supposedly lodged on his
head while he foraged for food. Safety
concerns forced officials to euthanize
the animal.

◆

A 44-year-old New Hope woman
purchased three white rats to prevent
them from being fed to snakes, which
ultimately resulted in her home being
condemned by health authorities.
Approximately 1,000 rats were
estimated to be in the home when it was
condemned in 1994.

Minnesota wood frogs freeze when they hibernate and thaw in the spring. They have developed physiological adaptations that help them survive being frozen.

◆

More than 5,000 zebra mussels were found in the trailer of a truck in 2007 when the vehicle was inspected in West Lakeland township. The mollusks are native to southeast Russia, proliferate quickly, and can disrupt the aquatic food chain. It is against Minnesota law to transport them, even if they are dead, as they were in this case. Company personnel did not realize that the mussels had attached to three pumps that had been recently removed

from a reservoir and were being hauled
back to the company that owned them.

◆

Mall of America aquarium workers
launched an emergency rescue mission
to save a reef shark in January 2008,
after a child alerted them that Jesse, a
300-pound sand tiger shark, had
chomped Little Shark 54, a smaller reef
shark, on the head. Workers maneuvered
a small boat to save Little Shark 54, who
received some cuts in the attack but no
major injuries.

◆

Home values near large animal feedlots
were surprisingly higher than those of

homes farther away, according to a July 1997, University of Minnesota study. The study was done to settle a dispute between the feedlots and their neighbors, who were objecting to the smell.

◆

Brainerd firefighters carried water-pump cans into the woods to put out a fire in a deer stand in November 2008. The stand caught on fire and a box of ammunition started exploding when the stand's portable heater fell over.

◆

Kandi Hanson has had several collisions with Minnesota deer. In 2007, she was running a 10-kilometer race when a deer ran into her. In earlier incidents, her car was damaged twice and totaled once.

◆

A deer jumped through a laboratory window at Minnesota's 3M headquarters in 2007 just as workers were starting their lunch hours. It broke beakers and made a mess of the lab before it escaped through a door left open by local police who responded to the incident.

◆

Spontaneous combustion reportedly caused potting soil in a flowerpot to burn, which melted the plastic in the pot, melted the plastic table on which it was sitting, caught a wooden deck on fire, and gutted a house in St. Paul in July of 2008. No one was injured in the blaze.

◆

The Como Zoo's 12-year-old twin polar bears, Neil and Buzz, are visiting three other polar bears that live at The Arctic Ring of Life exhibit in Detroit until their home is finished being renovated.

◆

Minnesota's state flower, the pink-and-white lady's slipper, can live up to 50 years and grow 4 feet tall. It can take up to 16 years for one to produce its first flowers.

Minnesota's Terry Nowacki has been developing horse-scent training since 2000. After training, the horses become sniffers to help search for missing people. According to Nowacki, horses can detect human scents up to 1,000 feet away.

◆

Oswald's Bear Ranch, the largest bear-only ranch in the United States, became the new home of a mother bear and her two cubs that had chosen to hibernate under a Minnesota cabin. The bears' capture involved a chase and a tree being cut down to recover a cub seeking safety in its branches.

Pesky gophers prompted two Minnesota towns to offer a gopher bounty to residents capturing or killing the pests. The town of Scandia set their bounty at $2 per gopher, while May township offered a $1.50 gopher bounty. Scandia eventually discontinued its bounty and decided to spend taxpayer dollars in other ways, but May's bounty still stands.

◆

In 2007, Henry the mule was Rod Maday's transportation as he traveled from Minnesota to Wyoming to find a job. The 1,500-mile trip took him 45 days. Maday chose a mule as his mode of transportation because he had no driver's license and no money. When he was younger, Maday hunted raccoons on muleback, so he had some prior mule riding experience.

◆

A donkey was successfully rescued from an abandoned well in Underwood in September 2007, by firefighters who used a front loader to dismantle the well block by block. The donkey had fallen into the well after wandering onto a neighbor's property.

◆

A 6-month-old resident of Baghdad was flown to his new Minnesota home in October 2008 after 65,000 people signed a petition and Minnesota's

congressional delegation got involved.
Ratchet the dog was found in a burning
trash pile and rescued by a U.S. soldier,
SPC Gwen Beberg. The flight for
Ratchet and a handler was paid for by
Northwest Airlines and Operation
Baghdad Pups, who paid $5,000 for the
dog's security and trip incidentals.
Ratchet is now living with Beberg's
family.

A 1-ton bull that escaped from a St.
Paul stockyard in January 2008,
damaged a police squad car's door when
he sideswiped it. The bull also charged
at a police officer twice before being
cornered in an alley and destroyed.

A large portion of northern Minnesota's red and white pine trees, estimated to be up to 350 years old, escaped being logged because of an 1882 survey crew error that designated the area as part of Coddington Lake. The error preserved 144 acres of the Chippewa National Forest near Blackduck, known as the Lost Forty.

◆

The "chicken people" of Mankato have worked to pass a new city ordinance lifting the city's chicken ban, so they can raise a few chickens in their yards and collect fresh eggs. Tim Krohn of the *Mankato Free Press* described the scene painted by opponents of the ordinance as "a sort of chicken-induced Armageddon."

An 80-ton battery, the size of two tractor trailers, is being tested by two Minnesota companies to hold energy harnessed by the wind. The wind-to-battery technology is expected to be able to power 500 homes for 7 hours.

Una the Saint Bernard has been immortalized in the name of the Cuyuna Range of iron mines. Una's owner, Cuyler Adams, discovered the iron ore range in 1904 and named it by combining the first three letters of his own name with the name of his dog.

Minnesota's state bird is one of the oldest living bird species in the world. The loon, or great northern diver, species dates back between 50 and 80 million years.

Dive-bombing the salad bar and feasting on spilled nuts in the bulk foods section were two favorite pastimes of a pair of finches that lived in Maplewood's Rainbow Foods Store in 2006.

Maplewood's Home Depot store has been home to barn swallows who have learned to use technology. The birds have figured out how to open the store's automatic doors to get in and out while foraging for food to bring back to their nests. One time, after an owner locked the doors the birds swarmed him until he let them out.

◆

Federal Duck Stamp sales and import duties on ammunition and firearms have funded a $4 million, 18,000-acre expansion of Minnesota's Glacial Ridge National Wildlife Refuge. The growth will provide a waterfowl habitat for blue-winged teals, Canada geese, mallards, northern pintails, ring-necked ducks, and tundra swans.

◆

More than 57 times the usual number of great gray owls invaded Minnesota in 2005. Researchers believe the sudden influx may represent about one-tenth of the total U.S. population. About 300 hawk owls and 400 boreal owls were also reported following a rodent population crash in their normal forest habitats.

◆

Turtles race down Main Street in Longville every Wednesday during the summer, earning the town the nickname Turtle Racing Capital of the World. Turtles are provided for potential racers who arrive turtle-less.

CRAZY FAMOUS PEOPLE

Sinclair Lewis, who was born in Sauk
Centre, Minnesota, in 1885, won the
Pulitzer Prize for his novel *Arrowsmith*
but refused the award because it was
based on the "wholesome atmosphere of
American life," which *Arrowsmith* did
not represent.

Author Sinclair Lewis apparently had a sweet tooth. His favorite Christmas cookies were called "Sinful Christmas Cookies" because they included a shot of bourbon.

Movie star Judy Garland was born in Grand Rapids in 1922. Her favorite dinner was steak and kidney pie.

Famous writer and novelist F. Scott Fitzgerald, who was born in St. Paul in 1896, briefly worked on the script of *Gone With the Wind*.

In 1991, Michael Ravnitzky, a law student from St. Paul, began requesting FBI files on famous dead people. He requested more than 2,000 files, and the ones he received included those of Humphrey Bogart, actress Lauren Bacall, Wyatt Earp, Helen Keller, Norman Rockwell, and Babe Ruth.

◆

Time magazine's first Man of the Year issue was in 1927 and featured Charles A. Lindbergh of Little Falls, Minnesota. Lindbergh made aviation history when he made the first trans-Atlantic flight from New York to Paris on May 20-21, 1927.

Minnesotan Frank B. Kellogg served as U.S. Secretary of State in President Coolidge's cabinet. He was awarded the Nobel Peace Prize in 1930 for his work on the Kellogg-Briand Peace Pact, which was signed in 1928. He was also the recipient of the French Legion of Honor.

◆

As of 2007, 20 Nobel Prize recipients have had a connection to the University of Minnesota. Four of those were in physiology or medicine, six were in physics, three were in chemistry, one in literature, five in economic sciences, and one received the Nobel Peace Prize.

One Minnesotan has been appointed to the United States Supreme Court: St. Paul's Warren Burger became chief justice in 1969.

♦

Hubert Humphrey, who served as vice president of the United States from 1965 to 1969, became the first Minnesotan to be nominated as a presidential candidate in 1968. Before he became involved in politics, Humphrey was a pharmacist.

CRAZY SPORTS

During excavation of the Metrodome in downtown Minneapolis, bulldozers ran into a 250,000-pound granite rock that is believed to have been at the location for about 11,000 years. The rock was eventually moved to a Plymouth, Minnesota, bank, which named it Plymouth.

Nine of the 20-member "Miracle on Ice" 1980 U.S. Olympic hockey team were from Minnesota: Bill Baker, Neal Broten, John Harrington, Steve Janaszak, Mark Pavelich, Mike Ramsey, Buzz Schneider, Eric Strobel, and Phil Verchota. Two other team members, Steve Christoff and Ken Morrow, were not from Minnesota but attended college there. Coach Herb Brooks was from St. Paul. He played and later coached hockey at the University of Minnesota. The team defeated the Soviet Union's team 4-3 and won the gold medal, although the Soviets were considered the world's best international team.

◆

There are more golfers per capita in Minneapolis than any other city in

America. There are 36 golf courses and 3 golf simulators within 10 minutes of the Minneapolis area.

◆

Minnesota Twins announcer Halsey Hal was the first person to say "holy cow" during a baseball broadcast.

◆

Dave Winfield from St. Paul was never part of the minor leagues but instead went straight to the major leagues, where he was part of six teams. His home team, the Minnesota Twins, was his fifth, and the last team he actually played for. Winfield was a seven-time Golden Glove winner, hit 465 home runs, and was elected to the National Baseball Hall of Fame in 2001.

◆

In 1994, Dave Winfield was traded by the Minnesota Twins to the Cleveland Indians. In exchange for Winfield, executives from the Indians club bought dinner for executives from the Twins. At the time of the initial trade, a player was to be named, but the season ended early because of a strike. Winfield, who was in the last years of his 3,000-plus hit career, never played for the Indians.

◆

Minnesota Twins' Chuck Knoblauch was the batter in one of baseball's rarest plays, which was called twice during an 8-day period and once during spring training in 1991. The play, catcher's interference (with a batter's swing), was called against the same catcher, Texas Rangers' Gino Petralli, all three times.

◆

Archibald "Moonlight" Graham settled in Chisholm, Minnesota, after he played his one and only game of baseball in the major leagues in 1905.

◆

A baseball game between the Minnesota Twins and California Angels is the only event or game that has ever been postponed because of a tear in the

Metrodome's roof. That game was in April, 1983. The Metrodome's distinctive fabric dome roof is held in place by the air pressure generated by up to 20 fans inside the stadium. A load of more than 10 inches of snow caused the dome to partially deflate under the snow's weight just 48 days after its initial inflation in October, 1978. When a bolt snapped, a sharp piece of steel tore through the fabric, allowing air to escape and complete the dome's total deflation. It took about 4 days to re-inflate the roof.

◆

The Metrodome is the only facility in the world that has hosted two World Series, two NCAA Final Four Basketball Championships, and a Super Bowl.

Grandma's Marathon was not named for a grandmother who won a race. Rather, it was named for its first major sponsor, a Duluth-based restaurant chain called Grandma's. The annual June marathon has grown from 150 participants in its first race in 1977 to more than 9,000. Winners have included participants from Kenya, Russia, Tanzania, Kyrgyzstan, Venezuela, New Zealand, Canada, England, Moldova, Belarus, Ireland, Morocco, Ukraine, and the United States.

◆

The course record for Grandma's Marathon men's division is 2 hours, 9 minutes, 37 seconds. It was set by Dick Beardsley and has stood since 1981. The number two record was set in 1980 by

Garry Bjorklund. It is 53 seconds longer than Beardsley's number one. The half marathon that takes place the same day is named after Bjorklund, two-time Grandma's Marathon champion and 1976 Olympian from Duluth.

◆

John Wooden's legendary basketball coaching career is primarily known for the astounding streak of 10 national championships that he won between 1964 and 1975 as coach of the University of California Los Angeles (UCLA) Bruins. According to Wooden, when he committed to the job at UCLA, he had already decided to coach for the University of Minnesota

Gophers, but a snowstorm got in the way. As the story goes, Wooden was waiting for a call from Minnesota to verify that he could bring in his own assistant coach, Eddie Powell. If this staff issue was resolved to his satisfaction, Wooden planned to go to Minnesota. A snowstorm in Minneapolis prevented his contact there from being able to get to a phone and make the offer. With no snowstorm to prevent UCLA's call later the same evening, Wooden took that job, assuming that Minnesota could not work out the staff issue. Despite his initial decision in favor of the Gophers, Wooden honored his commitment to UCLA.

Bemidji is known as the Curling Capital of the United States. Both the men's and women's U.S. Olympic curling teams practice their precision sport, played on ice, in the town.

CRAZY SUNKEN TREASURES

The U.S.S. *Essex*, based in Minnesota, did not wreck but was burned by its owners. The Navy ship served for 3 years and was the oldest steam-powered vessel in the Navy fleet. The president of the Klatzky Iron and Metal Company, A.J. Klatzky, bought the

Essex for $400. After she was partially dismantled, 200 gallons of kerosene and oil were used to burn enough of the boat so that the bottom could be pulled ashore.

◆

Of the 350 shipwrecks estimated to rest under the surface of Lake Superior, 50 are believed to be in Minnesota's waters.

◆

The *Hesper* was lost to a 1905 storm when it was pushed into a reef by 60-mile-per-hour-winds. The 15-man crew escaped the battered boat just moments before it broke up, but only after a giant wave lifted the boat over the reef. The

Hesper's well-preserved remains are located in Silver Bay Harbor.

◆

The *Amboy* sank in Lake Superior twice. When it first sank in 1891, it was known as the *Helena*. It went down with a full load of coal after being struck by a steel steamer. The 17-year-old schooner was salvaged and refitted in 1892 as a tow barge and renamed the *Amboy*. It was loaded with coal and was on its way to Duluth when it was caught by the Mataafa Blow, a 1905 storm that destroyed or disabled 18 ships. The crew was rescued after 13 hours. The *Amboy* was valued at $10,000. Its remains currently lie on the beach just south of Sugar Loaf Cove.

A gale on October 29, 1896, broke the *Samuel P. Ely*, a wooden schooner-barge, from a tug and blew her across the harbor at Two Harbors, Minnesota. She finally laid to rest after colliding with the stone breakwater that was being built at the time. Area newspapers reported that the winds at the time of the accident were up to 50 miles per hour, and it was the "most furious gale that has visited this end of the Lakes for a decade." The *Ely* was named for one of the founders of the Minnesota Iron Company and had been instrumental in Minnesota's iron ore trade before it wrecked. Her 10-man crew was rescued after the wreck.

Lake Minnetonka is home to scuttled streetcar boats that were used to transport residents and visitors in the early 1900s. The seven TCRT fleet streetcar boats were outfitted to mirror their land-bound counterparts with woven, split-cane passenger seats, sliding glass windows, canary-yellow paint, and comparable capacity.

◆

The streetcar boat fleet became obsolete by the early 1920s with the increased use of automobiles. Debris, including red clay tiles, from Big Island Amusement Park's demolition was used to fill three of the boats before they were pumped full of water and sunk in Lake Minnetonka. One of the boats was outfitted as a tug, one as an excursion boat, and two were dismantled.

◆

The steamboat *Minnehaha* was formerly one of the streetcar boats that lay on the muddy bottom of the lake for 50 years before it was discovered, pulled from the lake, and restored in 1996. It now cruises the lake and docks at Excelsior, Big Island, and Wayzata during the summer from late May until mid-October.

CRAZY GEOGRAPHY

A Texas man put his canoe into the Mississippi River at St. Paul's Hidden Falls Regional Park in September of 2008 and lived a life-long dream by paddling down the entire river in 78 days.

Although Minnesota's state nickname is Land of 10,000 Lakes, there are actually more than 12,000 lakes in Minnesota that cover more than 8.4 percent of the state.

◆

One-third of the town of Orono is covered by water. Its total area is 25 square miles, and 9 miles of it is lake.

◆

Twenty-one of Minnesota's 87 counties are named after bodies of water. They are Big Stone, Blue Earth, Chippewa, Chisago, Clearwater, Cottonwood, Crow Wing, Itasca, Kanabec, Koochiching, Lac qui Parle, Lake, Lake of the

Woods, Otter Tail, Red Lake, Redwood, Roseau, St. Louis, Traverse, Watonwan, and Yellow Medicine.

◆

Ninety-one Minnesota lakes are named Long Lake.

◆

There is a 1,699-foot difference between Minnesota's highest point, Eagle Mountain (measuring 2,301 feet), and its lowest point (602 feet), on the shore of Lake Superior.

Of the 2,348 miles of the Mississippi River from its start at Lake Itasca to its end in the Gulf of Mexico, 575 miles can be followed through Minnesota.

◆

In 1951, Minnesota produced 82 percent of the nation's total output of iron, which totaled more than 89 million tons.

◆

University of Minnesota researchers believe that there may be parallels between water life on Mars and an iron ore mine spring in Minnesota's Iron Range. Both Mars and the mine have rimstone dams, and water is trapped in the 2.7-billion-year-old rock in the mine, which may have similar traits to the rock on Mars.

CRAZY PLACES

Digital trespassing has been outlawed in North Oaks, where residents own the roads and have legally prevented Google Maps from showing images of its streets and homes online.

The National Park Service's no smoking policy is in effect at Pipestone National Monument, where local American Indians quarry pipestone and demonstrate the making of sacred pipes.

◆

The Heritage Hjemkomst (pronounced yem-komst) Interpretive Center in Moorhead, Minnesota, is home to a Viking ship that sailed from Duluth to Bergen, Norway, in 1982. The ship's builder, Robert Asp, along with friends, family, and volunteers, completed the ship's construction in 1980. Its maiden voyage took place on Lake Superior.

A full-scale replica of the Hopperstad
Stave Church in the town of Vik, Norway,
has been carved as part of the
Hjemkomst Center in Moorhead.

◆

Plymouth, Minnesota, hosts an annual
Fire & Ice Festival in February that
includes basketball, bowling, and mini
golf, all played on ice.

◆

Plymouth was ranked number one on
USA Today's 2008 Best Places To Live
list. Minnesota had nine cities ranked in
the top 100 of the list.

More than 115 acres are used for Montevideo's 12 city parks, earning it the nickname City of Parks. Nine of the parks are in residential areas, with the remaining three along the Chippewa River.

◆

The "alphabet streets" of north and south Minneapolis are named for historical figures in United States history and cover the entire alphabet. The only exceptions to this are Queen Avenue, Xerxes Avenue, York Avenue, and Zenith Avenue, which are simply named with words that begin with *q*, *x*, *y*, and *z*.

Foshay Tower in Minneapolis was modeled after the Washington Monument and was the first skyscraper built west of the Mississippi River.

◆

Famous conductor John Philip Sousa not only attended the dedication of Foshay Tower in 1929, but he also composed a special march for the occasion, "Foshay Tower Washington Memorial March." For the piece, tower owner Wilbur B. Foshay wrote Sousa a check for $20,000. When the stock market crashed just weeks later, the check bounced and Sousa subsequently forbade playing of the music again until the debt was settled. When Sousa's estate was later paid for the composition, the ban was lifted.

Blue Earth, Minnesota, was named for the Blue Earth River, which surrounds the town. Blue-black clay is found in the river's banks, and the American Indian Dakota tribe named the river Mahkota, or "blue earth." An enormous statue of the Jolly Green Giant and the Green Giant memorabilia museum are popular Blue Earth attractions.

◆

While on the map it is known as Austin, more people recognize this Minnesota town as Spamtown, USA. Austin is home to Hormel foods, which produces the canned meat product Spam, making it the only town outside the Twin Cities area in Minnesota with a Fortune 500 company.

Embarrass, located on the Embarrass River, derives its name from the French word *embarras*, meaning "to hinder, confuse, or be complicated." Early French settlers found the area around the river difficult to maneuver.

◆

Sleepy Eye takes its name from a Dakota chief whose name was Ish Tak Ha Ba, which means "sleepy eyes" or "droopy eyelids."

◆

Norwegian settler Knud Olson Bergo is credited for naming the town of Black Hammer. Unfortunately, a fire burned much of the land around Bergo's home

and charred a hill nearby, as well. Bergo
claimed the hill looked very much like a
hill he remembered from Norway called
Sard Hammer, which translates to
"black hill." The English and
Norwegian words were combined,
resulting in the name Black Hammer.

◆

The town of Coin received its name
during the William Jennings Bryan free
silver debate of the late 1800s, when
Bryan attempted to remove the United
States from the gold standard, and
instead use silver to back U.S.
currency.

Climax takes its name from a late 1800s Climax Tobacco company ad.

◆

Six fictional GI Joe characters call Minnesota cities and towns their homes: Tripwire and Bazooka from Hibbing, High-Tech from St. Paul, Charbroil from Blackduck, Steam-Roller from Duluth, and Dart from White Earth.

CRAZY WEATHER

International Falls is known as the Icebox of the United States, but not without challenge. Fraser, Colorado, also claimed the name in the 1950s, and the two cities lived with an agreement between them about the use of the nickname. Finally, the United States Patent and Trademark office officially gave the name to International

Falls on January 29, 2008. Shortly after that was settled, International Falls recorded a new low temperature of -40 degrees Farhenheit, beating the old record of -37 degrees Farhenheit set in 1967.

◆

Police suspect that Minnesota's cold weather motivated thieves to steal a boiler furnace from a Mankato home in October, 2007. But the robbers were considerate enough to shut off the water valve, which prevented the home from flooding.

A Super Bowl halftime family tradition for one Buffalo, Minnesota family ended in 2007 with a teenage son being treated for second-degree frostbite. The family usually runs outside barefoot in the snow, and in 2007 it was 17 degrees below zero the day of the game.

◆

Due to cold weather, the Target Holidazzle Parade has been cancelled nine times since the tradition began in 1992. Parade-goers can usually experience the parade from heated seats and the Minneapolis skyways during the Friday, Saturday, and Sunday night parades that take place from the day after Thanksgiving until just a few days before Christmas. The parade's most recent cancellation occured in 2008, when the Minneapolis wind chill reached 20 degrees below zero.

◆

Lamberton's temperature changed 71 degrees in 24 hours on April 3, 1982, earning the record for the largest recorded temperature drop over a 24-hour period in the history of the United States.

◆

The cold winter of 1843 recorded some historic Minnesota weather phenomena: an annual mean temperature of 38 degrees Fahrenheit for the Twin Cities; 20 degrees Fahrenheit below average for both

February and March; a large comet sighted during the last half of March; and a delayed opening of Lake Pepin into May.

◆

A snowplow operator took a detour from clearing county parking lots to clear off a boat ramp in Crookston in December of 2008 and ended up in the frozen Red Lake River. The driver was helped out of the freezing water, but the John Deere loader he was driving stayed at the river bottom for several hours before it was pulled out. Unfortunately, the driver not only got wet, but he also got fired for the accident.

Minnesota has recorded snow as early as September 14, in 1956, and as late as June 4, in 1935.

◆

The towns of Beardsley and Moorhead are tied for the hottest recorded temperature in Minnesota: 114 degrees Fahrenheit. Both records were set in July with Beardsley's on July 29, 1917, and Moorhead's in July 1936.

◆

An April 2008 snowstorm dropped a recorded 18 inches in Pelican Rapids, 15.5 inches in Brandon, and 12 inches in Donnelly.

The Ice Dive Capital of the World is the title that leaders of the Active Life and Running Club would like to tag to the city of Excelsior. It's the home of the club's annual New Year's Day On It & In It Lake Minnetonka Ice Plunge.

◆

Swimmers have been taking the Ice Plunge into Lake Minnetonka since 1991. Temperatures for the 2008 plunge registered -16 with the windchill, but 689 swimmers jumped in despite the cold.

◆

Weather records for the past 30 years indicate that there are only five places in the United States that are almost guaranteed to experience a white Christmas. International Falls and Hibbing, Minnesota, are included on this short list. Other areas of northern Minnesota have a greater than 90 percent chance of experiencing snow at Christmas.

◆

Boiling water evaporating before it hits the snowy ground, bubbles freezing when blown outside, wet hair freezing outside, sledding on a frozen towel, and using a frozen banana as a hammer to pound a nail through wood are some of the videos on YouTube submitted by Minnesotans to prove just how cold it gets in the Land of 10,000 Lakes.

The Great Lakes commonly experience seiches, oscillations caused by wind that minimally shift the water level but can occasionally cause extreme water level drop-offs. A Lake Superior seiche in 1995 caused a 3-foot rise and fall of the water level in just 15 minutes.

◆

A Hugo man was shielded from flying debris in a 2008 tornado as he crouched in his home's hallway holding his cat and dog. The storm ripped off the bedroom doors in the hallway and placed them gently on top of him and his pets.

A tornado that touched down in Hugo in 2008 left more in its wake than damage and destruction. It left some strange sights as well:

- a tree filled with pink insulation tufts, where the leaves had been before they were stripped by the storm;
- toilet paper that never ripped despite being unwound, draped across a countertop, and rewound in the sink;
- and dishes of cat food and water untouched in a home that had its roof ripped away and sofas overturned.

◆

Minnesota's longest dry spell lasted 79 days and spanned two different calendar years. The towns of Beardsley, Canby, Dawson, and Marshall experienced the dry spell, which lasted from November 9, 1943, to January 26, 1944.

◆

Winds of 110 miles per hour were recorded in an August 20, 1904, tornado in Minneapolis.

◆

Wim Hof, also known as the Ice Man, can withstand freezing temperatures without the typical physical results such as frostbite, hypothermia, and even death. The Minnesota man has climbed Mount Everest in shorts, swum under the ice in the Arctic, and has run a marathon at the North Pole barefoot. In addition, he jumps into frozen lakes on a daily basis in the winter.

◆

August 2007 holds the record for maximum monthly rain total. Hokah experienced 23.86 inches that month, with 15.10 inches falling on August 19th of that year.

◆

A few winters without a lot of snowfall made it difficult for the North St. Paul Jaycees to build their traditional snowman during the city's Sno-Daze celebration. A permanent solution to the problem was raised in 1974 with the building of a 54-foot-tall stucco snowman, the world's largest, which is now used as the city's logo.

CRAZY CULTURE

A polka Mass is shown on a local television station in the Boundary Waters area of northern Minnesota. The service is basically the same as any other traditional Roman Catholic mass but features distinctive polka music.

A giant cherry poised on the end of a 5,800-pound spoon is a fountain sculpture, by Claes Oldenburg that stretches more than 50 feet across the Minneapolis Sculpture Garden. The sculpture is named *Spoonbridge and Cherry*.

◆

John Wayne declined the role of Marshal Matt Dillon on the television Western *Gunsmoke* and recommended his friend, Minnesota actor James Arness, for the part. Arness played Dillon on the show's entire run from 1955 to 1975.

Noel Neill appeared in three Superman movies in a 58-year span. She starred as Lois Lane in the 1948 *Adventures of Superman* movie, played Lane's mother in the 1978 *Superman: The Movie*, and played heiress Gertrude Vanderworth in the 2006 *Superman Returns* movie. Neill was born in Minneapolis in 1920.

◆

John and Judith Borger donated an amazing personal collection of 40,000 comic books, worth hundreds of thousands of dollars, to the University of Minnesota in the spring of 2008. The collection includes not only *Superman* issues from the 1950s, but also *Justice League of America*, *The Flash*, and *The Sandman* comics.

Best-selling author Neil Gaiman lives near Minneapolis. Gaiman has written children's books, short fiction, prose, short stories, comics, and novels. He also created and wrote *Sandman*, the first comic to ever be awarded a literary award. *Sandman* was a monthly DC Comics horror-weird series, and its #19 won the 1991 World Fantasy Award for best short story. Gaiman also won three Harvey Awards and the award for best writer.

◆

The 2007 Academy Award-winning film *Juno* was written by first-time screenwriter Diablo Cody, who began her writing career while living in the Twin Cities area.

Bob Dylan's *Modern Times* album sold 192,000 copies in the first week of its release in September 2006, making the 65-year-old Dylan the oldest person to ever launch an album in the number one spot on the music charts. Dylan was born in Duluth in 1941 as Robert Zimmerman.

◆

Artist Fritz Scholder was born in Breckenridge, Minnesota, in 1937 and was one-quarter Luiseno Indian, but grew up in a self-described "non-Indian" way. In a PBS documentary about his life, he was quoted as saying, "I succumbed to a subject that I vowed I would never paint: the American Indian." In December 2008, the Smithsonian's

National Museum of the American Indian organized an exhibit titled "Fritz Scholder: Indian/Not Indian" in both Washington, D.C. and New York. Another exhibit, "Fritz Scholder: An Intimate Look" was organized in Santa Fe, New Mexico, at the Institute of American Indian Arts Museum.

◆

Fritz Scholder's paintings include *Super Indian No. 2*, which depicts a buffalo dancer with beads around his neck, wearing a horned headdress, and holding a two-scoop ice cream cone in place of the traditional rattle in his hand. Another image from Scholder's collection of works is titled *Indian With Beer Can.*

A 20-foot-long, 16-foot-tall leather boot weighing 2,300 pounds was created by the Red Wing Shoe Co. to celebrate the company's centennial in 2005. The size 638.5 boot is the world's largest and can be seen in Red Wing at the Red Wing Shoe Company Museum when it's not on tour.

◆

Outrageously decorated ice fishing houses travel through Aitken on pickup trucks, wagons, tractor trailers, and other creative means during the annual Aitkin's World-Famous Fish House Parade, held on the day after Thanksgiving. Thousands of spectators celebrate the kick-off to the annual ice fishing season as the houses make their way toward one of the 365 frozen lakes surrounding Aitken.

A dead cat, a wall of player piano rolls, unopened Christmas gifts, and a 1937 lollipop tree are just some of the items that Edwin Krueger saved during his lifetime and then willed to the city of Wykoff as part of a museum collection. The apartment and Jack Sprat Food Store that housed everything he ever owned has been cleaned, organized, and is maintained by the ladies of the Wykoff Progress Club, who threw out six truckloads of trash during the cleaning process.

CRAZY PHENOMENA

Eighty-foot crop circles were found in a Fosston, Minnesota wheat field in the summer of 2008, and others were found in a field about 4 miles away. In some of the circles, the wheat was pressed in a clockwise direction, while in others it was pressed counterclockwise.

"When the algae starts to bloom, Stinky will be here soon," is a saying in Waseca about Stinky, the Clear Lake monster that reportedly is spotted (and smelled) only during the summer.

◆

Many believe that Lake Pepin's lake monster, Pepie, and Nessie, the famous lake monster of Loch Ness, are related because Lake Pepin and Scotland's Loch Ness are almost identical in size.

◆

A $50,000 reward is available to anyone who turns in a photo of Pepie the Lake Pepin monster to Minnesota's Lake City Tourism Bureau. Steve

Raymond, a Lake City gas station and bait shop owner, says he once took a photograph of the Lake Pepin legend but can't collect on the reward because he lost the photo.

◆

Residents of a Madison Lake house, built in 1888, have repeatedly found the night-light in their infant child's room to be inexplicably turned off, moved to the other side of the room, or simply unplugged at the same time, 3:12 a.m., every morning. Information on the house's deed indicates that a mother and child who lived in the house in the early 1900s may have died. The current residents believe the ghost of the mother may have thought the night-

light was a candle and was putting it
out to protect her child.

CRAZY LAWS

Minnesota women who impersonate Santa Claus may face up to 30 days in jail.

◆

In Duluth, animals are not allowed to sleep in bakeries.

Minnesota state law forbids the teasing of skunks.

◆

People in Minnesota may not cross state lines with a duck atop their heads.

◆

Mosquitoes are declared a public nuisance throughout Minnesota.

◆

It is illegal not to tip your hat as you pass a cow in Pine Island, Minnesota.

An Alexandria law prohibits a man from making love to his wife if his breath smells of onion, garlic, or sardines. If his wife asks him to brush his teeth, he is compelled by law to do it.

◆

Red cars are prohibited from driving down Lake Street in Minneapolis.

◆

All men driving motorcycles anywhere in the state must wear shirts.

◆

Every man in Brainerd is legally required to grow a beard.

It is illegal to sleep naked in the Land of 10,000 Lakes.

◆

All Rochester residents thinking of going for a swim must first check with the chief of police to have their swimsuit approved.

◆

All Minnesota bathtubs must have feet.

◆

Hamburgers cannot be eaten on Sunday in St. Cloud.

Virginia, Minnesota, prohibits residents from keeping their elephants on the street, but Wayland residents can park their cows on the street if they are willing to pay 3 cents per day.

◆

Double-parkers in Minneapolis can legally be put on a chain gang.

◆

It is illegal to stand around any building in Minneapolis without a good reason to be there.

In Blue Earth, children under the age of 12 may not talk on a phone unless supervised by an adult.

CRAZY CRIME

A fox urine-filled SuperSoaker water gun was used as a repellent for teenagers vandalizing private property in December 2008 in Kandiyohi County. Property owner Scott Wagar spotted the teens through his night vision goggles and fired the urine on them. The fox urine substance he used is typically used to repel garden pests.

Heidi Dalibor, a Grafton woman, was arrested in August of 2008 for overdue library books. Despite the repeated notices she received, Dalibor ignored the situation until police arrested her at her home for nonpayment of the fine on two paperback books. In addition to the $30 fine, the situation cost her $172 when her mom bailed her out.

A Maple Grove bank received flowers and a gift box in May 2007—delivered by limousine—from a customer who told the florist that the gift was because he appreciated the bank's good service. The box actually contained a fake bomb, and the unsuspecting limo driver was given money in a trash bag for delivery to the robber after the robber called the bank with instructions.

◆

Justin John Boudin, 27, allegedly yelled at a woman, hit her in the face, and also hit an elderly man who tried to intervene as Boudin waited for a bus on the way to his anger management course. He was later tracked down by information on homework papers found in the folder with which he hit the man.

◆

A Concordia College security guard's golf cart was pushed into a campus pond in 2007—by naked students. The officer found 50 to 80 students and recent graduates skinny dipping to celebrate graduation. When he tried to get them to leave the area, they responded by pushing his cart into the water.

◆

Uncle Al was identified as a burglar by the 2-year-old toddler he left in a car while he broke into a house in October of 2007. Officers responding to a St. Paul residence's burglar alarm found the child, along with stolen power tools belonging to his mother, in a car that had been abandoned by the babysitting burglar. The child told officers the identity of the man who had been with him.

A man from Andover, Minnesota, received a 9-month prison sentence when he proposed to his ex-wife on the *Jerry Springer Show* in May of 2007. Thomas Michael Glynn proposed to his ex-wife on TV and kissed her on the cheek following the proposal. She said she wanted him back, but Glynn had broken his probation by seeing her. He was at the time under a no-contact order because of his prior conviction for choking her. A Minnesota probation officer saw the show and had Glynn arrested.

◆

Fleeing from a police officer and motor vehicle theft were the charges against a Minnesota man who stole an undercover deputy's car. He stole the car to get home immediately after being released from a detox center.

Oak Park police were called in November 2008 when a prisoner due for release refused to leave the grounds of the Minnesota Correctional Facility–Oak Park Heights. The prisoner was concerned that he would be re-arrested because he had not served his entire sentence. He had been released and re-detained for violating the terms of his release just months prior to his permanent release date. Officers assured him that his entire sentence had been served and convinced him to leave.

Samuel Tilley, a 20-year-old motorcycle driver, received a ticket for speeding in Wabasha in October 2004. He was clocked driving at 205 miles-per-hour. Police believe this marked the highest speed for which a ticket has ever been given. Tilley, the son of a sheriff, was 140 miles over the 65 miles-per-hour speed limit. In addition to speeding, he was driving without a license.

◆

A Rochester man was arrested twice in 2007 for two separate incidents of exposing himself in public. He told the judge that a prescription drug he was taking to treat his restless leg syndrome caused him to commit the crimes.

In January 1997, police found a man in Austin, Minnesota, urinating on his car's door lock to melt the ice. At first, he was given a warning because he convinced police it was his car. The police returned just minutes later and gave the apparently intoxicated man a ticket for DUI.

◆

A wedding dress, two bridesmaid dresses, the mother-of-the-bride's wedding day jewelry, and an aisle runner for the ceremony were stolen in a car taken from a service station in Waite Park in 2007. The mother-of-the-bride left the key in the ignition to talk to someone and watched her car, containing the wedding accoutrements, be driven away.

A West St. Paul bank inside a food store was robbed twice in the same day in November of 2007. Police were called following the first incident, but the suspect had fled into the woods. Most of the policemen left, but one officer remained to speak with witnesses. By the time he went to his car for paperwork and returned to the scene, the second robbery had occurred.

◆

An employee at family-owned company, Cooperative Plating Co. in St. Paul stole 2.5 tons of silver—1 ounce at a time— over the course of 3 years. The silver was valued at more than $500,000. He stole the silver to fund a gambling habit and finally graduated to taking up to 138 pounds at a time.

In 2007, the city of Minneapolis became responsible for reimbursing almost $2.8 million in traffic fines that were paid by drivers whose vehicles were videotaped while running a red light. The owner of each car videotaped was automatically fined even though the driver of the car was not shown on the videos. Many of the $142 fines had to be reimbursed when car owners declared they were not driving their own car and should not be fined.

◆

A thief, the victim, and the witness to the crime were all arrested during an incident at Bloomington's Mall of America in March 1996. Police arrested a man for stealing a $1,400 gold chain

from another man's neck. The victim
was arrested when police found crack
cocaine in his pocket. The eyewitness
who helped police nab the suspect had
several outstanding warrants and was
also arrested.

A color-blind slot machine at Mystic
Lake Casino in Prior Lake could not
detect red-stained bills that were marked
with ink from an exploding dye pack.
The money had been stolen from a bank
near Minneapolis in November of 2007,
and the thief was using it to gamble on
slot machines the following January. The
thief had spent about $500 when an alert
employee spotted the unusual red bills.

Wayne Boniface and his wife, Kathie, were confronted by an intruder in their Duluth home in 2007. The man quickly told them that they were blowing his cover as a government agent by discovering him. The intruder grabbed the wife, and his shirt came off during the ensuing grapple with the husband. As the shirtless intruder continued his escape, the porch railing slowed him down. When Wayne grabbed him again, the intruder's pants, underwear, and shoes also came off to completely remove his cover. Police later apprehended the suspect, but there was no report about whether he was still naked.

White powder found in a deodorant container was determined not to be cocaine after Cornelius Salonis, a Shakopee resident, spent 2 months in jail in 2008 for possession of the substance. The powder originally tested as cocaine but those results were annulled by a later more comprehensive test. The man was released on the drug charges but then pled guilty to driving while intoxicated charge, the cause of his initial arrest.

◆

St. Louis Park police literally pulled a man over for driving drunk in 2007. The driver stayed asleep at the wheel while officers ran to the moving vehicle, grabbed the wheel to steer it from the wrong lane, shifted gears, guided the vehicle to a stop, and removed the key.

◆

St. Paul police followed Enca Ballard through a McDonald's drive-through to arrest her in December of 2008. The 26-year-old woman had just received her order and ate a few french fries before she was arrested for drunken driving after running a red light and ignoring police sirens and flashing lights. She thought they were after her because of her expired license and figured she might as well get her order before she was caught.

A $30 bet cost John Greely $750 in March 2008. A deputy watching from a boat launch in Silver Lake, Minnesota, saw an 18-year-old man running across a frozen lake dressed only in his socks. The man was reportedly sober and was charged with lewd and lascivious behavior. He had been challenged by his friends to perform the expensive stunt.

◆

A naked thief stole a bicycle from a female guest in a Minnesota hotel in November of 2007 and rode the bike down the hallway, knocking down two people. The thief also stole a pair of swim trunks, which he put on once he was caught.

In Minnesota, text messaging is not an advisable defense for reckless driving. A man who was subsequently arrested for driving drunk in 2008 claimed that text messaging caused him to drive into oncoming traffic and nearly collide with a deputy's squad car. The state's text messaging provision preceded the incident by about 48 hours.